DUBLIN

Donated to

**Visual Art Degree
Sherkin Island**

D0178109

An Introduction to

Ironwork

Plate 1
Medieval blacksmiths at work; a detail
from *The Romance of Alexander*
Painting on vellum
Flemish, 1338-44 by Jehan de Grise
On the right the smith wields an enormous hammer and a lump of iron rests
on the anvil. In the middle is the
forge, apparently double-sided. The
coals rest on a glowing surface, and
are fanned by two sets of bellows
which are powered by some invisible
means, possibly mechanical. Heaps of
spare fuel lie under the forge. On the
left another smith sits at a work-bench
covered with saws and files.
Oxford, Bodleian Library, ms. Bodley
264, fo. 164 v.

COVER
Trivet
Wrought iron
English, 18th century
l. 40 cm (15¾″) w. 33.6 cm (13¼″)
580-1905

FRONT ENDPAPER *(left)*
Grille from the Chantry Chapel of
Henry V, Westminster Abbey: detail
Wrought iron, carved, with pierced
sheet iron
English, 19th-century copy of the
original, made by the Royal blacksmith Roger Johnson 1425-31, and still
in situ.
1888-426

FRONT ENDPAPER *(right)*
Gate to the Choir of Canterbury
Cathedral: detail
Wrought iron, carved and riveted
English, 19th-century copy of the
early-14th-century original still in
situ.
1912-2

Fig. 1
Casting iron
Engraving
French, from Diderot's *Encylopédie ou Dictionnaire raisonné des sciences des arts et des métiers,* Vol. IV, section 3, pl. 5, Paris, 1765
The preparations for different casting operations are schematically shown. In figs. 1 and 2 of the illustration the sand is being packed into a flask for a closed mould, and in fig. 3 weights are being placed on the flasks (which probably contain several moulds) prior to pouring in the iron. In fig. 4 an open mould is being prepared: a fireback pattern is being pressed face down, into the sand; another such pattern is shown at Y.

Plate 2 (opposite)
Weather-cock
Iron and copper, embossed and painted
French, early 18th century
Weathercocks were in use in England well before the Norman Conquest, but were not produced on the Continent until much later. They almost invariably took the form of a cock and were often gilded.
h. 1.27 m (4′ 2″) w. 87.6 cm (2′ 10½″)
909-1906

An Introduction to

Ironwork

Marian Campbell

Assistant Keeper, Department of Metalwork,
Victoria and Albert Museum

LONDON: HER MAJESTY'S STATIONERY OFFICE

ILLUSTRATIONS

The colour plates and black and white figures have been numbered independently. The captions are ordered from left to right starting at the top of an illustration.

Whereas the text figures have been positioned as closely as possible to their references, the colour plates are in chronological order and the figures that follow them have been arranged thematically.

Copyright © Marian Campbell 1985
First published 1985

Series editor Julian Berry
Designed by HMSO Graphic Design
Printed in the UK for HMSO

ISBN 0 11 290415 7
Dd   718123   c65

To N.L.R.

LEABHARLANNA ATHA CLIATH
COLLEGE OF MARKETING
ACC. NO.   0112 904157
COPY NO.   MT 1001
INV. NO.   1491
PRICE IR£   6.70
CLASS
              739.4

ACKNOWLEDGEMENTS

I would like to thank the many friends and colleagues from whose advice and help I have benefited in compiling this little book. The photographic challenge was considerable, as will be appreciated by all who have themselves attempted to photograph ironwork, or merely to manoeuvre it into place. I am therefore especially grateful for photographic and other assistance from Christine Darby, Mike Kitcatt, Marjorie Trusted, Eric Turner, Jonathan Voak and Jeremy Whittaker.

M.C.
June 1984

PHOTOGRAPHIC ACKNOWLEDGEMENTS

B.T. Batsford Ltd figs. 34, 37, C. Blair fig. 20, Bodleian Library pl. 1, British Museum figs. 3, 48, A.F. Kersting fig. 9, Elmar Ludwig fig. 28, National Monuments Record figs. 14, 37, National Museum of Wales fig. 52, Albert Paley fig. 55, Warwick University, History of Art Dept. figs. 69, 70.

HER MAJESTY'S STATIONERY OFFICE
Government Bookshops
49 High Holborn, London WC1V 6HB
13a Castle Street, Edinburgh EH2 3AR
Princess Street, Manchester M60 8AS
Southey House, Wine Street, Bristol BS1 2BQ
258 Broad Street, Birmingham B1 2HE
80 Chichester Street, Belfast BT1 4JY
Government Publications are also available through booksellers
The full range of Museum publications is displayed and sold at
The Victoria & Albert Museum, South Kensington, London SW7 2RL

Introduction

Iron is the most plentiful metal on earth, but it is neither extracted nor worked with ease. Until the late Middle Ages the only known method of working iron in Europe was to forge or hammer it, to produce wrought iron. With the subsequent adoption of the blast furnace it became possible to melt the metal so that it could be poured into moulds and so produce cast iron.

By the early 19th century cast iron had become the dominant form; it was so easily and cheaply available that it was decoratively used and misused in superabundance. The result has been that iron is still today tarred with disfavour, and too rarely associated with beauty. Yet much ironwork, and especially wrought iron, consists of bold patterns and linear designs of great graphic power and aesthetic appeal.

Wrought iron readily lends itself to elegant eccentricities of design and so is highly suitable for gates, balconies and balustrades; cast iron, on the other hand, is better for repeating patterns, such as railing uprights, and for designs in relief. The visual effect of much ironwork was often originally enhanced by colour and gilding, for gates and staircases, locks and chandeliers were rarely the dismal black they are now painted. The techniques used in the production of both cast and wrought iron have always exerted a great controlling influence on their design, with the result that it is often difficult either to date pieces, or to attribute them to a particular area very precisely.

2

Fig. 2
Mask from the Fountain Garden, Hampton Court: detail of the back
Wrought iron, embossed
English, by Jean Tijou c. 1693
Lent by the Dept. of the Environment

Production of iron

Pure iron is extremely rare in nature, except in the form of meteorites. It is most commonly found in the red earth known as iron ore, from which the metal can only be extracted by applying intense heat. In the direct smelting method, used in Europe from c. 500 BC to 1500 AD, charcoal and iron ore were heated together to a temperature of c. 1200°C. This produced, when cool, a 'bloom' or lump of iron mixed with impurities, which were then removed by hand hammering. The result was wrought iron, a fairly pure form of the metal, light grey in appearance and with a pronounced woody grain. It can be freely shaped — hammered, bent, split, twisted, cut or stretched — whether hot or cold. The iron becomes harder and more brittle with hammering, but annealing (heating and then slowly cooling) returns it to its original state. By definition, wrought iron can only be forged, and it is the material mostly used by blacksmiths until very recently.

Furnaces at their most primitive consisted of depressions in the ground or stone shafts. These soon developed into cupola-shaped furnaces made of fired clay, and gradually increased in size. A major technological advance was made in Europe in the late 14th century with the development of the blast furnace, in which a very high temperature could be obtained by using water power to drive huge bellows. This caused the iron to become molten and incidentally to absorb some of the carbon from the charcoal fuel. The liquid metal was then run off from the furnace and channelled directly into moulds in the form of, say, firebacks, or into intermediary moulds known as pigs.

The high carbon content (2.2%-5%) of cast or pig iron makes it hard and too brittle to be forged — it shatters if hammered — but allows it to melt readily and to be recast. Although useless to the blacksmith, it is ideal for the mass production of identical objects. A purer and forgeable iron is made by smelting the cast iron pigs in a finery, in order to remove the carbon and other impurities — a process known as the indirect smelting method.

During the 17th century an increasing shortage of wood and hence of charcoal prompted experiments, particularly in Germany and England, to produce iron with an alternative fuel, coal. In c. 1710 Abraham Darby in Coalbrookdale, Shropshire, made one of the earliest successful attempts, having first converted the coal into coke. The gradual adoption of coke as *the* furnace fuel helped to facilitate the enormous expansion of the iron industry in the late 18th and 19th centuries. Further technological advances subsequently improved the processes of refining the iron, and brought down its price.

LIBRARY
College of Marketing & Design
Ph. 742721

Leabharlann Atha Cliath

5

Steel was only produced in Europe in small quantities until the 19th century, and was used primarily for weapons and edged tools. Consisting of iron with some carbon content, its great properties of hardness and elasticity were created by artificial means. Mild steel, with characteristics very like those of wrought iron, and containing no more than 1.5% of carbon, was not produced until 1856 when Henry Bessemer invented a process which removed the carbon from the pig iron in its molten state. Mild steel can be wrought or cast, and is the material most commonly used by blacksmiths today, while in industry it is used in the manufacture of bridges, cars and ships.

Ironworking techniques

Wrought iron

Wrought iron is forged by the blacksmith on an anvil. From time immemorial the smith's essentials have been a forge in which to heat the iron, a water tank in which to cool it, a hammer, tools and an anvil. Set on a wooden block which acts as shock absorber, the most commonly used type of anvil has a flat top surface and is horn-shaped at one end and blunt at the other. It is used as a solid base for hammering the heated iron into shape, and for welding and for chiselling, while curved shapes can be made on its pointed end. Let into the blunt end, known as the *heel,* are differently shaped holes — the round *pritchel-hole* that simply allows a punch to be driven through iron that is on the anvil, and the rectangular *hardie-hole* that serves to secure fixed anvil tools. The most common of these fixed tools are *stakes* (miniature anvils for producing various special shapes in the metal), the *hardie* (a wedge shaped chisel used for splitting hot metal and for cutting lengths), and *swages* (simple dies with their upper and lower parts used for finishing convex shaped rods and finials).

In addition to these, the modern smith uses powered tools. Perhaps the most important is the electric *power-hammer,* with interchangeable top and bottom dies (in effect hammers and anvils). Although hammers powered by mechanical means (at first water, and later steam) have been in use since medieval times for large-scale operations, the modern electric power-hammer has revolutionised the size, quantity and decoration of the work a smith can produce single-handed. Very recently smiths have also adopted the use of the oxyacetylene cutter, which has long been used in heavy industry. Its high temperature flame burns the metal locally, and enables the smith to cut substantial thicknesses very quickly — incidentally producing decorative effects not otherwise

obtainable. Some smiths today also use the *fly-press* or the more powerful *hydraulic press:* with either of these, single precise forming operations can be carried out with cold or hot dies.

The classic and simplest way to join two pieces of iron is to weld them by heating both to a high temperature and hammering them together until they fuse. Other methods include *collaring* (encircling the parts to be joined with small metal collars), *mortising* (as in carpentry), *riveting* and *screwing.*

Most wrought iron designs consist of a simple interplay between various forms of scrollwork and straight elements, whether plain, twisted or angled. Techniques used to add further decorative variety include:

BLUEING — the surface of iron or steel is heated up until it glows and then quenched (plunged in water), when it becomes blue in colour, the shade varying according to temperature. The technique is used for its decorative effect and because it helps to inhibit rust.

CARVING — the iron is carved cold in exactly the same way as stone or wood.

DAMASCENING — the art of encrusting gold, silver or copper wire on the surface of iron or steel. A pattern is traced onto the surface of the metal, and finely undercut with a sharp instrument. The wire is then forced into these minute furrows by means of hammering. The term is derived from Damascus, the city whose early goldsmiths are supposed to have pioneered the technique.

EMBOSSING (or repoussé work) — the art of raising ornament in relief from the reverse side (fig. 2). The design is first drawn on the surface of the metal and the motifs are outlined with a tracer, which transfer the essentials to the back of the plate. This is then embedded face down in pitch on a block and the portions to be raised are hammered down into the pitch. Next the plate is removed and re-embedded with the face uppermost. The hammering is continued, this time forcing the background of the design into the pitch. A series of these processes is finally followed by chasing.

Cast iron

Components essential for producing a piece of cast iron are a pattern, a mould, and the founding or casting process itself (fig 1). The pattern is usually of wood, plaster of Paris or metal; precision is needed in making it to take account of the shrinkage of cast iron when cold.

The mould is made of different types of sand or earth and packed into an iron frame known as a flask. The sand can be green (wet) or dry. Two types of mould — open and closed — are used; the former for simple one-sided objects like firebacks, the latter for complex shapes. In the case of an open mould the pattern is pounded with a sledge-hammer into sand set in a frame on the foundry floor. It is then removed, and apertures made in the mould: the sprue through which the molten metal is poured, and the risers for the escaping air.

Closed moulds can be made up of one or more parts which fit together to enclose the iron completely. To minimize weight and cost, complex castings are often hollow. For this a core mould is used — that is, another mould placed inside the closed mould.

The metal is heated until molten and poured into the moulds; once cool, the shape of casting is fixed. Unlike cast bronze, which allows additional chasing and polishing, little more can be done to cast iron.

Surface finishes

In most climates iron begins to rust as soon as it is smelted from its ore, and needs some sort of protection. In the medieval period wrought iron could be varnished, dipped in pitch, or tinned, as well as painted and gilded. In 18th century England, and probably also on the Continent, wrought ironwork seems frequently to have been gilded and painted blue, and sometimes green or white.

In the 19th century ironwork was sometimes brightly painted or given a bronze finish, but it seems that the fashion, still prevalent, of painting iron black, may have begun in the latter part of the century. Nowadays other possibilities are to wax it, to galvanize it with zinc and then paint it, or simply to leave it with a layer of rust.

Early history

The early history of iron-working has been obscured by the paradoxical nature of the metal: strong yet prone to rust. Unprotected iron objects rust away and decay entirely in a very few years. As a result there are few well preserved remains of the products of the blacksmiths of antiquity, which were predominantly weapons and tools.

Some iron beads of c. 3500 BC, found at Jirzah in Egypt, appear to be amongst the earliest known wrought iron artefacts, but they are made of meteoric iron. The technique of extracting iron from the ore seems to have been mastered by at least 2800 BC, to which date can be ascribed fragments of a wrought iron dagger blade found at Tall al-Asmar in Mesopotamia. However, the first real iron industry was probably not established in Asia Minor until between c. 2000 and 1500 BC. The knowledge of iron production and working spread slowly from the Middle East westwards to Greece, probably by c. 1000 BC, and so to Europe, reaching the British Isles in about 500 BC. The Chinese were from a very early date — the 6th century AD

at least — skilled in the production of cast iron, not known in the West until the late Middle Ages, but they apparently did not make wrought iron. This may well indicate that their discovery of the metal was independent, and not the result of western influence.

Iron seems at first to have been rare and considered by some to have semi-magical powers. Once iron had become comparatively easily obtainable it appears to have been used not only for weapons and tools but for everyday items. A number of Celtic firedogs survive from northern Europe, such as one from the 1st century AD in the National Museum of Wales in Cardiff (fig. 52). Like several others, it is dramatically decorated with elaborate terminals in the shape of ox-heads.

The Romans on the other hand appear to have used decorative wrought iron sparingly. Iron rings were given, according to Pliny, as tokens of engagement in the 1st century AD. Otherwise iron window-grilles are known from Pompeii and Herculaneum, as well as from British sites. The plain 4th century window grille from the Roman villa at Hinton St. Mary, Dorset, now in the British Museum (fig. 3), combines effective functionalism with simple form.

Complex decorative ironwork is not generally found before the Middle Ages, either because it was not made, or because it has perished. Perhaps more typical of the

3

Fig. 3
Window grille from Hinton St. Mary, Dorset
Wrought iron
Roman, 4th century AD
Rare in being comparatively intact. Found on the site of a Roman villa
h. 54.5 cm (21½″) w. 61 cm (24″)
British Museum Dept. of Prehistoric & Romano-British Antiquities no. 1966, 2-6, 1

pre-medieval period is the highly practical but intricate cauldron suspension-chain, dating to the 7th century, found at Sutton Hoo, Suffolk, and now in the British Museum. It is made up of plain loops which interlock with others shaped as the horns of stylised rams' heads.

The Middle Ages

One of the commonest medieval uses of ironwork was for the protection of wooden doors and chests (plates 9 & 10 and figs. 36 and 37). All needed strengthening, and elaborate hinges were designed which covered much of the surface and acted as both hinge and guard. One of the earliest pieces in the V&A is the 12th century hingework saved from the derelict St. Alban's Abbey in the 19th century. Here the hinges are decorated with S-shaped scrolls, an elaboration upon the C shapes most common at this date. More angular motifs can be seen on the 13th century doors from Gannat in the Auvergne in France (fig. 36). Hinge scrollwork could be enormously elaborate, and was often stamped with dies of different patterns, such as on the late 13th century door at Merton College Oxford (fig. 35). England is particularly rich in its collection of medieval doors and chests with elaborate ironwork, many still surviving in the places for which they were made (figs. 34 and 37). However some of the most intricate stamped scrollwork hinges ever made were those designed for Notre Dame Cathedral in Paris in the 13th century. Although 19th century copies now ornament the doors, parts of the originals are preserved in the Musée de Cluny, Paris.

Grilles might be very simple like the 13th century examples still in Canterbury and Lincoln Cathedrals, consisting of back-to-back C scrolls held together by 'collars', or be rather more varied, like the screen from Chichester Cathedral, now in the V&A (fig. 15) but in a sadly dilapidated state; its original appearance was enhanced by red paint. Complex designs — transformed from a scrolling motif into flower-terminals — can be found on 13th century grilles: for instance those in the Museum of Antiquities in Rouen, in Winchester from St. Swithun's shrine (fig. 16), or in situ still in French and Belgian churches. A famous and elaborate example of stamped scrollwork is the grille which still guards the tomb of Eleanor of Castile (d. 1296) in Westminster Abbey. This, unusually, has the added distinction of having a known maker, Thomas de Leghtune (probably Leighton Buzzard, Bucks) who was paid £12 for making, transporting and installing the grille.

Another much used motif was that of the quatrefoil (cluster of four petals) found in screens and grilles all over

Fig. 4
Chapel screen in the Palazzo Publico, Siena: detail
Wrought iron
Italian, by Nicolo di Paolo 1436
The cut-out cresting and elaborate quatrefoil motifs are characteristic at this date. The frieze includes scenes of Romulus and Remus suckled by the wolf.

Europe; rare dated examples can be seen in Italy (fig. 4), in Orvieto Cathedral (1337) and Santa Croce in Florence (1371). Floral or leaf-shaped terminal-motifs cut out from sheet iron appear to have been in use as early as the 12th century in Germany: gates so decorated can be seen in Hildesheim Cathedral. Commonplace by the 15th century, these devices continued in use well into the 16th century, and are seen most often decorating the tops of tomb railings.

In the 15th century blacksmiths began imitating the motifs that were being produced by their contemporaries, with rather more ease, in wood and stone. This necessitated much cold carving of the iron, a laborious and difficult technique. The gates still in place around the chantry of Henry V (d. 1422) in Westminster Abbey demonstrate the remarkable three-dimensional effect which could be achieved by overlaying complex geometrical motifs (front endpaper *left*). Their maker was the King's blacksmith, Roger Johnson, of London. Later in the century, c. 1483, another royal blacksmith, John Tresilian, made the screen and gates for Edward IV's chantry chapel with the same difficult technique. Though devoid of their original gilding, they can still be seen in St. George's Chapel, Windsor.

An aspect of door furniture, as well as of security, for which iron was well suited and used from an early date, is of course the lock. Locksmithing was always a specialist side of blacksmithing requiring extreme patience and skill, since it demanded both cold cutting of iron, and great precision. The V&A collection contains a number of ornate Gothic locks and keys from doors and chests from all over Europe (plate 16). One of the most ornate locks still boasts its original gilding (plate 4) and is entirely Gothic in style, though it was made for Henry VIII, that essentially Renaissance King. It comes originally from a royal manor, Beddington House in Surrey, and is probably by the King's locksmith Henry Romains.

Iron had long been used purely functionally in architecture to join or support timber. However, apart from screens and gates, which were both decorative and yet integral to a building, iron was not widely used in the visible architecture of the early medieval period. Such things as iron balconies seem only to appear in the 14th

5

Fig. 5
Balcony from Casa Bartolomeo, Venice
Wrought iron
Italian (Venetian), 14th century
Made up of a series of quatrefoils linked together by iron collars
h. 89 cm (2′11″) l. 1.65 m (5′5″)
Lent by the City Museum and Art Gallery, Birmingham

century — first, perhaps, in Italy. An example on loan to the V&A comes from the Venetian palace, Casa Bartolomeo (fig. 5). Decorative minor architectural fittings were also being made in 14th century Italy: dog-nosed wall-brackets and hooks, door-knobs and handles, can still be seen on the walls of houses in Siena and Florence.

In the domestic sphere, iron long served for such items as candlesticks (fig. 65) and, more rarely, chandeliers (plate 3), whilst its most important uses were in connection with the fireplace and with cooking (plate 11). Firedogs and firebacks, cauldrons, spits, trivets (see cover) and chimney-cranes were all made of iron, and were all as decorative as they were efficient at performing their functions. Most surviving examples are impossible to date with precision — for instance, a number of wrought iron firedogs in the V&A (fig. 53) are of Gothic design but very probably date from well into the 16th century. Almost none of the spits and cauldrons depicted in medieval manuscripts survive, but it seems that they differ little in overall design from their 18th-century counterparts.

The one vital novelty of the late medieval period was the introduction of cast iron. It was first used in Europe in the late 14th century for military purposes, principally the making of cannon. It was possibly, at first, only as a sideline that the foundries which produced these also made firedogs, stoveplates, and firebacks — themselves an innovation in the 15th century when fireplaces with chimneys had only recently come into fashion. The V&A has a good collection of firebacks dating mostly from the 16th and 17th centuries, in which English examples predominate. These are often said to have been made in the Weald in Sussex, which had since Roman times been an important ironworking centre. However other parts of the country, notably the Forest of Dean, had reputations as ancient for the production and working of iron, and there is no reason why many firebacks should not rather be attributed there.

The most famous of the V&A collection is the 'Armada' fireback (fig. 57) although there is nothing except its date, 1588, and the nautical motifs, specifically to link it with the attack. The fireback (fig. 61) depicting an oak and the initials 'CR' probably commemorates Charles II's famous escape after the battle of Worcester by hiding in an oak tree. Political themes seem also to have been popular on Continental firebacks. Firedogs (figs 53 and 54) were made all over Europe in cast as well as wrought iron, which it largely superseded. This was partly no doubt because cast iron was cheaper to produce, and partly because its fire-resistance was found to be greater than that of wrought iron.

In Germany and Scandinavia freestanding cast iron stoves were popular, often being of three or four tiers, made up of several stove-plates rivetted together. These, like firebacks, tended to be moralising, or to show Biblical scenes, such as Moses and the brazen serpent, the feast at Cana (fig. 59), or the Crucifixion. There are several odd stove-plates in the collection, but it lacks any complete stoves, and these must be looked for in their countries of origin.

16th & 17th centuries

Even in Italy Renaissance motifs were slow to find their way into the blacksmiths' repertoire. However, the simple elegance of a pair of 16th century window grilles (fig. 33) is in shape and style undoubtedly post-Gothic, as are the ebulliently baroque embossed figures on the 17th-century staircase balustrade, also Italian (fig. 45). This would no doubt originally have been brightly painted and gilt rather like the ornate Spanish panels (plate 6) of about the same date. Known by the Spanish as *plateresco*, that is 'in the manner of a silversmith', the technique — one undoubtedly more suited to metals softer than iron — demanded great skill from the smith. The Spanish were prodigious users of decorative ironwork from at least the 15th century, and unsurpassed in the 16th century. Huge *rejas* (screens) from this period still adorn many of their churches and cathedrals, as in Barcelona, Burgos, Seville and Granada. Some are as much as thirty feet high, often embellished with colour, gilding and silvering. These screens usually incorporate balusters skilfully decorated by means of cold carving, which despite its difficulty was apparently a popular technique with Spanish smiths. Large parts of *rejas* from Avila Cathedral are in the V&A, and date from between the late 15th and the 16th century (fig. 23).

The considerable versatility of Italian smiths in the 17th century is demonstrated in the screen (Mus. no. 231-1890) and grille (fig. 17) in each of which flat ribbon-like strips of iron are used, but to very different effect. Rare oddities in the collection are the Venetian gondola prows, also 17th century, of engraved wrought iron (plate 7); the diarist John Evelyn noted such prows on his visit to Venice in 1645. Although no longer found on gondolas today, elaborate prows are depicted as early as the 15th century, descendants perhaps of the animal-headed examples shown on the ships in the Bayeux tapestry.

North of the Alps, blacksmithing in the 16th and 17th centuries showed equal skill, though rather different in style. The heavy Flemish window grille of the early 16th century from Ghent (Mus. no. 5975-1857) is largely Gothic in design, consisting of massive spiked iron bars decorated with somewhat incongruous dog-like creatures at the terminals. A German grille of a beguilingly simple design — bars arranged in a lozenge pattern — proves on closer inspection to be a technical tour-de-force (fig. 6); see the complexity of threading and turning. The design of three German window grilles of the 17th century made for St Nicholas's Church, Aachen (fig. 30) seems by contrast, charmingly light-hearted. The use of round sectioned bars, the trick of threading one bar through another, and the scrolling design are marked characteristics of German blacksmithing of this period, and are features often found in work as late as the end of the 18th century.

6

Fig. 6
Grille from Jacobskirche, Aachen: detail
Wrought iron
German, 16th century
The simple design conceals the complex skill needed to produce it
h. 78.7 cm (31″) w. 56 cm (22$\frac{1}{8}$″)
1000-1893

An aspect of wrought ironwork peculiar to southern Germany and Switzerland is the effect of architectural perspective. It was often created in huge church screens by means of piercing sheet iron to a pattern of receding columns, as in the screen in the V&A from Constance Cathedral in Switzerland (fig. 7). Probably by Johann Reifell, it dates from c. 1646 and, though now black, it was originally painted in light blue and gold. Many of these screens are still in place, and can be seen in the cathedrals of Lucerne and Zurich, and in the abbey church of Muri in Switzerland, in the church of St. Ulrich in Augsburg, W. Germany, and — transplanted — at Powerscourt, Co. Wicklow, Ireland. Also characteristic of southern German blacksmiths' work of this period are

Fig. 7
Screen from Constance Cathedral
Wrought iron
Swiss, by Johann Reifell c. 1646
Reifell also did work in Zurich and in Lucerne
Cathedrals
h. 3.7 m (12′5″) w. 3.8 m (12′6″)
57-1890

Fig. 8
Puzzle padlock
Steel
German, 17th century
If the studs on the face of the padlock are correctly arranged, the steel hands holding the key will rise up and release it. Two turns of the key are necessary to lock or unlock, and in each unlocking an indicator at the back moves forward one point on a circular dial. If, in locking, the key is turned three times, unlocking becomes impossible until a certain knob is correctly turned and pulled
l. 23 cm (9″) w. 13.4 cm (5¼″)
M 8-1932

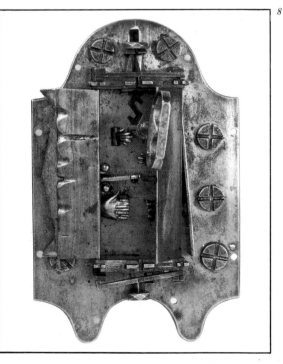

8

elaborate and whimsical gutter spouts, of which the V&A possesses a dragon and a devil (plate 8) as well as intricately worked grave-crosses.

The specialist skill of locksmithing was one at which Germany excelled and the V&A possesses many outstanding examples (fig. 8). Perhaps the height of elaboration in a lock can be seen in the so-called 'Armada' chest (plate 9), where the lock mechanism entirely covers the inside lid of an iron chest. Numerous examples are known of these chests which were produced in southern Germany, particularly in Nuremberg, from c. 1600-1800 and exported to all parts of Europe. Their name presumably arises from the mistaken belief that they were intended to hold bullion for the financing of the Spanish Armada, and that they were washed up in England from the wrecked Spanish ships.

The Gothic style long persisted in France. However a school of locksmithing grew up under the royal patronage of Francis I (d. 1547) and Henry II (d. 1559) which produced highly complex locks, keys and caskets in brilliantly polished chiselled iron. Amongst these, most famous is the 'Strozzi' key (plate 16) which is alleged to have been made to allow Diane de Poitiers, Henry II's mistress, entry to the King's private apartments. The bow (the loop forming the handle) is made up of two grotesque figures back to back, a design typical of many late 17th century French keys. The superb gates of c. 1650 to the Galerie d'Apollon in the Louvre, made originally for the château of Maisons-sur-Seine, are technically akin to locksmithing being of polished chiselled steel.

A renaissance in architectural ironwork was encouraged by Louis XIII, who succeeded to the throne in 1610, and was himself an amateur blacksmith. For the rest of the 17th century the craft now blossomed in France, responding to a need for ironwork in the large numbers of newly-built mansions and palaces, parks and gardens. Among many famous ironwork designers were Jean Berain, Daniel Marot and Jean Lepautre; characteristic to all is a fondness for symmetrical scrollwork with repoussé embellishments, and the use of square sectioned bars that are riveted together. Work of this period can best be seen in situ: at Chantilly, Fontainebleau, St. Cloud and above all, Versailles. The V&A has very few examples (fig. 38).

In England the shrugging off of a Gothic style was equally hesitant. The gates of 1525-33 to Bishop West's chantry chapel in Ely Cathedral show a lingering fondness for the Gothic, in their use of ogee arches, coupled with an attempt at a naturalistic floral design that is more Renaissance in spirit (fig. 14). Similar motifs decorate chandelier suspension-rods, such as a 17th century example in the V&A (plate 5), whose three-dimensional design is enhanced by the remarkable survival of its original colour and gilding. From the end of the 17th century, the gates and window-grilles below the Wren Library in Trinity College, Cambridge, by the London smith, Partridge, retain vestiges of this floral motif combined more prominently with symmetrically placed C-scrolls of classic simplicity. They herald much of the wrought ironwork of England in the 18th century.

By contrast comes the lush exuberance of the work of Jean Tijou, who is renowned above all for the numerous screens and gates he made for William and Mary for the Fountain Garden at Hampton Court. Made between 1689-96, they cost £2160 2s 0½d — including the iron and workmanship — a fabulous sum at the time. They can still be seen at Hampton Court, and a number of fragments from them are on loan to the V&A (figs. 19-21). Tijou is a somewhat mysterious figure — a Protestant Frenchman who left France after the revocation of the edict of Nantes in 1685, came to England in c. 1687 and left in c. 1712, at which point records of him cease. Other examples of his work survive at Burghley House, Stamford, and in screens in St Paul's Cathedral. They all make much use of repoussé work, apparently the first use of this

technique on iron in England. Tijou was however a lone star, and left no real successors.

The 18th century

All over Europe this was a golden age for blacksmiths, whose skills were needed to provide the increasing numbers of the prosperous with screens and gates for their parks, and staircases and balconies for their houses. Many are still to be seen in place in England, particularly in Oxford (fig. 24) and Cambridge, but few retain their original gilding and dark blue or sometimes green or white paint. Throughout the century the design of English wrought iron was a restrained blend of symmetrical motifs, of uprights, water-leaves and C-scrolls (fig. 24). The embossed work of Tijou was not practised on so luxuriant a scale by his successors, though the fine early 18th-century work of Robert Bakewell as at Melbourne, Derbyshire (fig. 9), and of the Davies brothers of Wrexham, shows a distinctive tempering, with embossed motifs, of the classical repertoire of uprights and C-scrolls.

Elsewhere in Europe characteristic native styles continued to flourish. In German-speaking areas blacksmiths' work is found in abundance; it is notable for a continuing use of elaborate foliage and interlaced bars whose curving forms flow with extraordinary plasticity. However the most exciting innovation of the century was the riotous symmetry and asymmetry of the Rococo style, conceived in France in the 1720s. French and German blacksmiths in particular were inspired to produce in iron marvellous and paradoxically lightweight effects (fig. 40) undoubtedly enhanced originally by colour and gilding.

The Rococo style was scarcely adopted by British smiths. French work in this style can best be seen in situ, as in the gates and screens by Jean Lamour in the Place Stanislas in Nancy. One of the few French examples in the V&A is the balcony of c. 1770 from a house in Versailles (fig. 39), decorated with baskets of fruit and flowers and with the arms of the Blacksmiths' Guild of Paris as its central motif. The collection also contains German pieces of great virtuosity.

Towards the end of the 18th century the revival of the Classical style brought an elegance and restraint to the design of ironwork. A building boom in cities all over Europe coincided with the availability of cast iron. It was suitable, in a way that wrought iron could never be, for casting into the newly-fashionable neoclassical motifs, and it was much cheaper because of recently-improved production methods. In England cast iron had first been

were made by the Carron Company foundry in Stirling-shire. In some cases wrought and cast iron could be combined to good, and no doubt economical, effect, as in the gates from Lansdowne House, London (Mus. no. M1-1961). Elsewhere in Europe, although change was soon to come, the use of wrought iron continued to flourish.

The 19th and 20th centuries

In Europe, north of the Alps and Pyrenees, the 19th century witnessed the flowering of cast iron as the principal material for gates and railings, which could now be mass-produced. Wrought iron was in the eclipse, being more costly to produce and laborious to work. Such was the enthusiasm for cast iron, with its chameleon-like ability to assume the form and appearance of almost all other materials, that it was used for impractical or bizarre purposes: aquaria (back end-paper), water-troughs and even jewellery (fig. 10).

Fig. 10
Bracelets
Cast iron
German, made in Berlin by the Prussian Royal Foundry
c. 1830
The Foundry, established in 1804, specialised in producing small articles such as plaques, snuff-boxes and jewellery – work now known as 'Berlin iron'. These were widely exported, and inspired imitations by French and German factories. The fashion for iron jewellery was encouraged by the Prussian War of Liberation, of 1813-15. Patriotic Prussians handed over their gold jewellery and wedding rings, in exchange for which they received cast iron jewellery sometimes inscribed 'Gold gab ich für Eisen'.
32–1888
(a) l. 18.6 cm ($7\frac{1}{4}$") w. 6.2 cm ($2\frac{1}{4}$")
(b) l. 22.5 cm ($8\frac{3}{4}$") w. 4.6 cm ($1\frac{3}{4}$")
Circ. 172–1917

Fig. 9
The arbour at Melbourne Hall, Derbys
Wrought iron, embossed
English, by Robert Bakewell of Derby, 1707-11
Bakewell (b. *c.* 1675, d. 1755) was an important smith of his generation. This is one of his earliest known commissions; other examples of his work can be seen at Okeover Hall, Staffs., All Saints Church, Derby and the Radcliffe Camera, Oxford.

used architecturally early in the century. Railings around St Paul's Cathedral in London of c. 1710-14, of which the V&A has a section, and those around the Senate House in Cambridge of c. 1730 (fig. 26), all show in their size and shape a debt to the design of cannon, which formed the principal product of the iron foundries of the day.

In the late 18th century the architect brothers Adam produced graceful designs in cast iron: stoves (fig. 47), fireplaces (fig. 49), railings and balconies (fig. 41), which

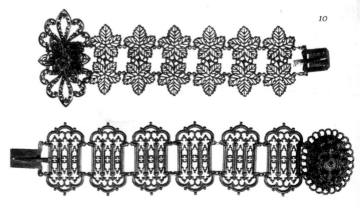

10

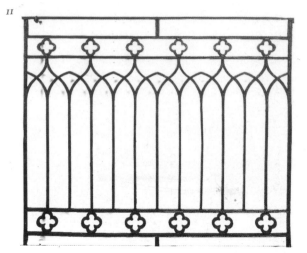

II

12

Fig. 11
Balcony panel from Torrington Square, London
Cast iron
English, c. 1830
Similar designs appear in both the Carron Co. catalogue of 1824 and *The Smith's and Founder's Director* (1824) by the architect L.N. Cottingham, but it remained popular, and is still being reproduced today.
h. 91.5 cm (3′) w. 1.2 m (3′11″)
M 1-1962

Fig. 12
Garden seat
Cast iron
English, made by Coalbrookdale & Co. c. 1860
Known as the 'Medallion' pattern
h. 1.02 m (3′4½″) w. 1.67 m (5′5½″)
M 6-1979

And similarly in architecture, càst iron now often masqueraded as something else: stucco in the Doric columns of Nash's Carlton House Terrace arcade in Pall Mall, London, of 1829-33, or carved stone in the Coal Exchange in London of 1847-9 (now demolished) built

by J. B. Bunning, of which the V&A has several sections (fig. 71). Where cast substituted directly for wrought iron it at first took on similar slender forms (fig. 11), so that it is sometimes hard to distinguish between the two. Soon however bolder designs appear, using three-dimensional modelling. The garden bench (fig. 12) of c. 1860, could only have been made in cast iron, and contrasts with the garden seat of c. 1800 in wrought iron (fig. 13). This, though graceful, is laboured in construction, and might have been more neatly cast.

By the middle of the century, a reaction against the use of cast iron is evident, pioneered by architects who drew their inspiration from the Middle Ages. Figures such as Viollet-le-Duc in France, and Sir G. Gilbert Scott in England (fig. 22) did much restoration work on medieval churches and cathedrals, in the course of which they renewed or replaced the wrought iron screens that had earlier been swept away. At the London International Exhibition of 1862, various firms showed examples of wrought ironwork in styles which aped the Gothic and the Renaissance. In England the philosophical principles of A.W.N. Pugin (1812-52), John Ruskin (1819 1900) and William Morris (1834-96), who all hated modern methods of production, including cast iron, inspired the Arts and Crafts movement. The revival of artistic craftsmanship which followed led to the use of wrought iron once more for domestic items like candlesticks, firedogs (fig. 53) and fire-irons, with designs that often harked back to the 17th and 18th centuries.

Between c. 1890 and 1914, the emergence of the sinuous organic forms of the Art Nouveau style stimulated much imaginative architectural work in both cast and wrought iron. The most exciting of this was on the Continent: in cast and wrought iron by Victor Horta (1861-1947) in Brussels (fig. 70) and Hector Guimard (1867-1942) in Paris (fig. 43), the designer most notable for the railings and lamp-standards of the Metro; in wrought iron by Alessandro Mazzucotelli (1865-1938) in Milan, and Antonio Gaudí (1852-1926) in Barcelona. In Britain the outstanding figure is Charles Rennie Mackintosh (1868-1928), an architect who designed wrought ironwork of great originality for his buildings in and around Glasgow (plate 19). Each city still retains some of these masterpieces, but much has been wantonly destroyed.

The First World War marked the beginning of a long period of decline in the architectural use of all types of ironwork. However in the 1920s large quantities of wrought iron were still being produced by Edgar Brandt in Paris and Samuel Yellin in Philadelphia. Brandt (1880-1960) produced work characterised by the geometric motifs of 'Art Deco' combined with stylised fruit and flowers (figs. 53b and 68); Yellin (1885-1940) was more eclectic and ranged in style from the neo-Gothic to the neo-Georgian. In the 1920s and 1930s cast iron was also being used all over Europe for the grilles and gates needed for the spate of new buildings being erected.

Fig. 13
Garden chair
Wrought iron, originally painted dark green
English, early 19th century
h. 91.5 cm (3′) w. 51 cm (1′8″)
W 11-1977

The Second World War brought to an end this building activity, and the attendant demand for ironwork. If it had not, no doubt the new requirements of the Modern Movement in architecture — which eschewed ornament — would soon have done so. Doubtless because of this change in architectural fashion, post-war building activity was not accompanied by an interest in the decorative uses of ironwork. Only since c. 1970 has there been any sign that wrought ironwork at least might find a place in the decoration of a modern building. In this renaissance, Achim Kühn of East Germany can be seen as a pioneer; his gates for the 1958 Brussels World Fair helped to inspire a generation of smiths. Today the most remarkable work seems to be that of Manfred Bergmeister of West Germany (fig. 28), Antonio Benetton of

Italy and Al Paley of the USA (fig. 55), while in Britain the conservatism of the blacksmithing tradition has recently been shrugged off (fig. 51). One of the most striking examples of English modern ironwork is the pair of gates in forged stainless steel designed and made by Tony Robinson (1981-3) for the medieval Great Hall in Winchester. In many of these pieces modern tools, notably the power-hammer, have been used to achieve novel effects.

Buildings as recent as the National Westminster Bank Tower in London and Lever House in New York are bare of decorative detail; certainly embellishment with ironwork would hardly suit their severely functional style of architecture. Yet it is hardly a century since 1889, when the Eiffel Tower opened, constructed from 9,000 tons of wrought iron. The architectural novelty of its day, it was for years the tallest building in the world, and is a potent reminder of the structural and aesthetic possibilities of the metal. While another such triumph is perhaps unlikely, the bold designs recently produced in wrought iron may inspire architects of the future to use decorative ironwork in new buildings as well as old.

The scope of the collection

The V&A's earliest recorded purchase in any material was of a pair of German 17th century wrought iron hinges, bought in 1844, and the bulk of the ironwork collection was acquired between the 1850s and the 1890s. The V&A's ironwork collection is the largest in Britain and one of the most comprehensive in the world, ranging in date from the 12th century to the present day. It is enormously diverse and includes both the expected — items of domestic and architectural use, grates, gates, firebacks, candlesticks, chests, locks, keys and tools and the unexpected — furniture and jewellery.

The V&A's policy in the 19th century was to collect only 'old' ironwork — almost exclusively wrought iron — and to ignore the great variety of decorative cast iron being produced at the time. Consequently the principal glory of the collection is still the wrought ironwork, especially of the period between the 16th and 18th centuries; although the range of 16th and 17th century cast iron firebacks and firedogs is good, the post 1700 cast iron collection is as yet extremely sparse.

The original V&A buildings themselves incorporated a good deal of decorative ironwork, and although most was cast — the staircase balustrading, the fine grill in the old restaurant (plate 18), ornate radiator panels and the restaurant tables designed by the sculptor and designer Alfred Stevens — some wrought iron was also used; for

instance the gates (fig. 27) which then led to the mews where the Museum horses were stabled. But much has unfortunately been swept away in the course of successive schemes to modernise the Museum.

Recently however the Museum has commissioned several pieces of new wrought ironwork: gates to the recently opened Cole Wing (1981-2) by Christopher Hay, gates to one of the entrances to the Ironwork Gallery, almost entirely made with a power-hammer (1981-2) by James Horrobin, and a remarkable chandelier in steel, coloured with neoprene (1983-4) by David Watkins for the Silver Galleries.

The ironwork in the Museum is however mostly seen at a double disadvantage: divorced from its original setting, whether of stone, brick or wood, and stripped of its original colours. When acquired in the 19th century many pieces are recorded as being painted and gilded, but the fashion of the time dictated that this be obliterated by a uniform black paint. Nevertheless, the Ironwork Gallery of the Museum remains as much a place of fascination today as when described in 1900 by H.G. Wells, in his novel *Love and Mr Lewisham*:

"As one goes into the South Kensington Art Museum from the Brompton Road, the Gallery of Old Iron is overhead to the right. But the way thither is exceedingly devious and not to be revealed to everybody, since the young people who pursue science and art thereabouts set a peculiar value on its seclusion. The gallery is long and narrow and dark, and set with iron gates, iron-bound chests, locks, bolts and bars, fantastic great keys, lamps, and the like, and over the balustrade one may lean and talk of one's finer feelings and regard Michael Angelo's horned Moses, or Trajan's Column (in plaster) rising gigantic out of the hall below and far above the level of the gallery."

Further reading

Some of the books below themselves have useful bibliographies, indicated *(B)*. Books in print are shown *(P)*.

Ayrton, Maxwell, and Silcock, Arnold, *Wrought Iron and Its Decorative Use*, London, 1929. A history of wrought iron with examples of British work (excellent photos).

Blanc, Louis, *Le Fer Forgé en France aux XVI et XVII Siècles*, Paris and Brussels, 1928.

Blanc, Louis, *Le Fer Forgé en France. La Régence: Aurore, Apogée, Déclin*, Paris and Brussels, 1930. Amongst the best surveys of French ironwork.

Bossaglia, Rossana, and Hammacher, Arno, *Mazzucotelli: L'Artista Italiano del Ferro Battuto Liberty*, Milan, 1971. A large-format photographic essay on the work of this important art-nouveau Italian ironworker.

Borsi, Franco, *Victor Horta*, Brussels, 1970. Illustrations of the work of an important Art Nouveau designer of ironwork.

Byne, Arthur, and Stapley, Mildred, *Spanish Ironwork*, New York, 1915. Thorough.

Chatwin, Amina, *Cheltenham's Ornamental Ironwork*, Cheltenham, 1975. The only guide to the 18th and 19th century ironwork, mostly cast.

Clouzot, Henri, *La Ferronnerie Moderne*, Paris, 1928. Many photos of interesting Art Deco ironwork.

Cottingham, L.N., *The Smith's and Founder's Director, Containing a Series of Designs and Patterns for Ornamental Iron and Brass Work*, London, 1824. Contains many designs for cast and wrought ironwork.

D'Allemagne, Henry-René, *Histoire du Luminaire*, Paris, 1891. Copiously illustrated.

D'Allemagne, Henry-René, *Les Anciens Maîtres Serruriers et leurs Meilleurs Travaux*, Paris, 1943. Valuable illustrations.

Ferrari, Giulio, *Il Ferro nell' Arte Italiana*, Milan, 2nd ed. 1923. An Italian text illustrated by many of the best examples of Italian craftsmanship.

ffoulkes, Charles, *Decorative Ironwork, from the XIth to the XVIIIth Century*, London, 1913. Excellent historical review, illustrated by many famous examples.

Frank, Edgar, *Old French Ironwork*, Camb., Mass., 1950.

Geerlings, Gerald Kenneth, *Wrought Iron in Architecture*, New York and London, 1929 *(B)*. Examples and discussion of techniques; excellent illustrations of American and European work.

Gloag, John, and Bridgwater, Derek, *A History of Cast Iron in Architecture*, London, 1948 *(B)*. Misleadingly entitled for it is one of the best accounts of cast iron, covering all types of object, and well illustrated.

Haedeke, Hanns-Ulrich, *Metalwork*, London and New York, 1970. A useful account.

Harris, John, *English Decorative Ironwork from Contemporary Source Books, 1610-1836*, London, 1960. A selection of drawings from original source books, including Tijou's 'A New Booke of Drawings'.

Hollister-Short, G.J., *Discovering Wrought Iron*, Tring, 1970. A short but excellent guide. Illustrated.

Henriot, Gabriel, *La Ferronnerie Moderne*, Paris, 1923.

Hoever, Otto, *A Handbook of Wrought Iron from the Middle Ages to the End of the Eighteenth Century*, London and New York, 1962. Includes good photos of European work.

Jones, A.C., and Harrison, C.T., 'Cannock Chase Ironworks 1590' in *The English Historical Review*, 93, 1978, pp. 795-810. The earliest contemporary English description of the complete process of iron-making from the raw materials to the production of bar iron.

Kauffman, Henry J., *Early American Ironware, Cast and Wrought*, Rutland, Vermont, 1966. Useful.

Kühn, Fritz, *Decorative Work in Wrought Iron and Other Metals*, London, 1967 reissued 1982 *(P)*. Consists mainly of photographs, working drawings and captions, exploring the wide range of Kühn's work.

Lindsay, John Seymour, *An Anatomy of English Wrought Iron*, London, 1964. Remarkable drawings of details and techniques of English ironwork.

Lindsay, John Seymour, *Iron and Brass Implements of the English House*, London, 1964, *(P)*. Excellent drawings of a comprehensive range of domestic ironwork.

Lister, Raymond, *Decorative Cast Ironwork in Great Britain*, London, 1960, *(B)*. Good technical information on cast iron and useful photos and drawings.

Lister, Raymond, *Decorative Wrought Ironwork in Great Britain*, London, 1957, reprint Newton Abbot, 1970. A very good introduction to tools, materials and techniques, followed by a historical survey of British ironwork.

Mainwaring-Baines, J., *Wealden Firebacks*, Hastings, 1958, *(P)*. The only survey of firebacks in print. Useful.

Malchenko, M., *Art Objects by Tula Craftsmen*, Leningrad, 1974. Well illustrated account of the steel furniture produced at Tula.

Martinie, H., *La Ferronnerie: Exposition des Arts Décoratifs, Paris, 1925*, Paris, 1926. Useful on 1920s ironwork.

Meilach, Dona Z., *Decorative and Sculptural Ironwork*, New York, 1977, *(P)*. Largely non-architectural ironwork. Very good photos. Text sometimes technically unreliable.

Needham, Joseph, 'Iron and steel production in ancient and medieval China' in *Clerks and Craftsmen in China and the West*, Cambridge, 1970, (Chapter 8).

Raistrick, Arthur, *Dynasty of Iron Founders: the Darbys of Coalbrookdale*, Newton Abbot, 1970. The best account of the pioneering Darbys.

Robertson, Edward Graeme, and Joan, *Cast Iron Decoration: A World Survey*, New York, 1977, *(B)*, *(P)*. Photos of cast iron and an excellent survey.

Schroeder, Albert, *Deutsche Ofenplatten*, Leipzig, 1936. German stove-plates discussed and illustrated.

Schmidt, Eva, *Der Preussische Eisenkunstguss*, Berlin, 1981 *(P)*. 18th and 19th century cast iron in N. Germany, including Berlin iron jewellery.

Schubert, H.R., *History of the British Iron and Steel Industry c. 450 BC — 1775 AD*, London, 1957. The classic account.

Sonn, Albert H., *Early American Wrought Iron*, New York, 1928. Pencil drawings which include tools, gates, and balconies.

Southworth, Susan and Michael, *Ornamental Ironwork*, Boston, 1978, *(B)*, *(P)*. An excellent survey of the design, history and use of cast and wrought iron, particularly in American architecture.

Starkie Gardner, J., *English Ironwork of the 17th and 18th Centuries*, London, 1911, facsimile reprint: New York, 1976. The classic account of the best period of English ironwork written by a practising smith.

Starkie Gardner, J., *Ironwork*, London, HMSO 1922-30 reprinted in 1978 (3 volumes) *(B)*, *(P)*. An excellent survey although not all attributions are reliable: illustrated mostly from the V&A collections.

Straker, Ernest, *Wealden Iron*, London, 1931.

Stuttmann, Ferdinand, *Deutsche Schmiedeeisenkunst*, Munich, 1927-30. Many photos of German wrought iron.

Tylecote, R.F., *A History of Metallurgy*, London, 1976, *(B), (P)*.
A detailed and scholarly account of the technology of iron.
Untracht, Oppi, *Metal Techniques for Craftsmen*, London and New York, 1968. Useful practical guide, well illustrated.
Zimbelli, Umberto, and Vergio, Giovanni, *Decorative Ironwork*, London, 1966. Short general survey, well illustrated.

Exhibition & Museum Catalogues

Carbondale, Illinois Southern University at Carbondale 1976: *Iron Solid Wrought/USA*. The work of American smiths, 1776-1976.

Dusseldorf: Kuratorium Kunstausstellung 1952: *Kunstausstellung Eisen und Stahl*.

Houston, Texas, University of St. Thomas 1966: *Made of Iron*.

Krefeld, Museum Burg Linn 1982: *Eisen statt Gold*. Prussian cast ironwork, including jewellery.

Lindau, Bodensee 1969, and subsequent years: *Kunstschmiede-arbeit Heute, (P)*. Modern wrought ironwork.

London, Victoria & Albert Museum 1982: *Towards a New Iron Age: the art of the blacksmith today, (B), (P)*.

Ontario, Art Gallery 1975: *Wrought Iron: European Household Utensils from the 17th to the 19th Century*.

Paris, *Le Fer à l'Exposition Internationale des Arts Décoratifs Moderne*, 1re et 2e Séries, by Guillaume Janneau, Paris 1925.

Rouen, Musée le Secq des Tournelles, *Ferronnerie Ancienne*, Henry-René d'Allemagne, 2 vols, Paris, 1924. Illustrations of the best wrought iron collection in the world.

Sheboygan, Wisconsin: John Michael Kohler Arts Center, 1980: *The Metalwork of Albert Paley*.

Toulouse, Musée Paul Dupuy 1966: *La Serrurerie du XIVe au XVIIIe siècle*. Useful discussion and illustrations of locks.

Washington D.C., Dimock Gallery of the George Washington University, 1971: *Sketches in Iron: Samuel Yellin, American Master of Wrought Iron, 1885-1940*, Myra T. Davis.

Welsh Arts Council, Cardiff, 1977: *Davies Brothers, Gatesmiths*, Ifor Edwards. A study of the 18th century Welsh smiths.

Museums to visit

A selection of those with good, often specialist, collections of ironwork, or technical displays. Those indicated * also contain collections of designs, and † libraries with relevant books and catalogues; those indicated ‡ have particularly outstanding collections.

BELGIUM

Bruges	Gruuthusemuseum
Brussels	Musées Royaux d'Art et d'Histoire

FRANCE

Avignon	Musée Calvet
	Musée Bricard
Paris	Musée Carnavalet
	Musée de Cluny
	Musée des Arts Décoratifs

Rouen	‡Musée le Secq des Tournelles
Troyes	Maison de l'Outil et de la Pensée Ouvrière

GERMAN DEMOCRATIC REPUBLIC

Dresden	Historisches Museum

FEDERAL REPUBLIC OF GERMANY

Munich	Bayerisches Nationalmuseum
Nuremberg	Germanisches Nationalmuseum

GREAT BRITAIN

Amberley, W. Sussex	Chalk Pits Museum
Cambridge	Cambridge and County Folk Museum
Cardiff	Welsh Folk Museum, St. Fagan's
Edinburgh	Royal Scottish Museum
Guildford	Guildford Museum
Hastings	Hastings Museum and Art Gallery
Ironbridge, Salop	†‡Ironbridge Gorge Museum
Lewes, Sussex	Anne of Cleves house Museum
London	British Museum
	Museum of London
	†Science Museum
	*†‡ Victoria and Albert Museum
Reading	Museum of English Rural Life, Reading University.
St. Albans	City Museum

NORWAY

Oslo	Norsk Folkemuseum, Bygdøy

SPAIN

Vich	Museo Arqueológico Artístico Episcopal

SWEDEN

Lund	Kulturhistoriska Museet
Stockholm	Nordiska Museet
	Statens Historiska Museet

UNITED STATES

Carbondale, Illinois	Southern Illinois University at Carbondale
Chicago	Art Institute
Landis Valley, Pennsylvania	The Pennsylvania Farm Museum
New York	*The Metropolitan Museum of Art (including The Cloisters)
	*The Cooper-Hewitt Museum
Philadelphia	Philadelphia Museum of Art
St. Louis	St. Louis Art Museum
Winterthur, Delaware	The Henry Francis du Pont Winterthur Museum

USSR

Leningrad	The Hermitage

LIBRARY
College of Marketing & Design
No. 742721

Illustrations

3

4

Plate 4
The Beddington lock
Iron, wrought, carved and gilded
English, probably made by Henry Romaynes between 1539
and 1552
This door-lock was originally that of the main door to the
great hall of Beddington Place, Surrey, held by the Crown
between 1539 and 1552. The arms are those used by all Tudor
monarchs, especially Henrys VII and VIII. Henry Romaynes
held the post of lockmaker to both kings, but was also a blacksmith. It is likely that a lock now in the Walters Art Gallery,
Baltimore, and a pair of firedogs at Knole House, Kent, are
also his work.
h. 23 cm (9″) w. 34 cm (13½″)
M 397-1921

Plate 3
Chandelier
Iron, wrought and gilded
German, 15th century
Chandeliers at this date were more commonly of brass, no
doubt because it could be mass-produced and was therefore
cheaper.
h. 95.3 cm (3′1½″) w. 49.5 cm (1′7½″)
5990-1857

Plate 5 (right)
Chandelier suspension-rod
Wrought iron, painted and gilded
English, late 16th century
h. 2.3 m (7′8″) w. 1.1 m (3′7″)
876-1868

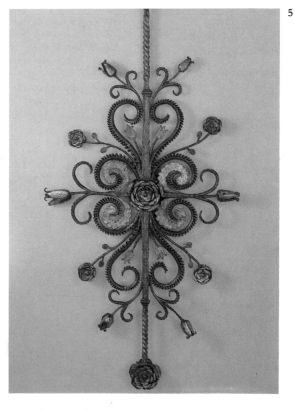

5

6

Plate 6
Detail of a panel from a screen
Iron, embossed and painted
Spanish, 16th century
Whole h. 22.3 cm ($8\frac{3}{4}''$) w. 1.01 m
($3'3\frac{7}{8}''$)
M 429-1927

9

7

Plate 7
Gondola prow
Wrought iron, polished and engraved
Venetian, 17th century
There is a similar example also in the
collection, and another in the Metro-
politan Museum, New York
h. 1.2 m ($3'11''$) w. 57 cm ($1'10\frac{1}{2}''$)
9091-1863

Plate 8
Gutter – spout
Iron, embossed and painted
German, 18th century
h. 1.17 m ($3'10''$) w. 66.5 cm ($2'2\frac{1}{4}''$)
1210-1872

Plate 9
Armada Chest
Wrought iron, painted; the lock of
steel, engraved
German (Nuremberg), 17th century
The name 'Armada Chest' is applied
to a distinctive type of coffer, made of
wrought iron strengthened with
interlaced bands of the same material,
of which large number are in exist-
ence. As here, in most examples the
lock, often elaborately engraved,
occupies the whole of the inside of the
lid and generally has eight bolts which
catch under the in-turned edges of the
sides. There is often an imitation key-
hole in front, the real one being con-

8

cealed in the lid, and sometimes two
or more staples for padlocks. Many
examples were originally painted but
this rarely survives.
The term 'Armada Chest' does not
seem to have been current before the
middle of the 19th century. It presumably originated in the erroneous
belief that these coffers were designed
to hold bullion for the financing of
the Spanish Armada, and that they
were subsequently washed up on our
shores from the wrecked ships. The
theory is negated by the fact that most
examples are considerably later in date
than the Armada. The chests were
made in all sizes, from a few inches in
length, intended for jewellery, to five
or six feet in length, suitable for a
banker's reserve. They served as the
forerunners of the modern commer-
cial steel safe. Large numbers were
made in southern Germany, particularly in Nuremberg, from the end
of the 16th century until the last
quarter of the 18th century, and
exported to all parts of Europe. Their
design varies little, and it is rarely
possible to date any with precision.
h. 48 cm ($1'7''$) w. 47 cm ($1''6\frac{1}{2}''$)
l. 91.5 cm ($3'$)
4211-1856

Plate 10
Caskets; all were for jewellery or valuables

(a)
Wrought iron, backed with red cloth
French, 15th century
h. 10 cm (4″) w. 19 cm (7½″)
M 640-1910

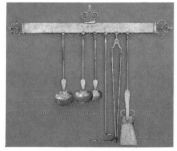

Plate 11
Rack of cooking implements
Steel, wrought and polished, and cast brass
Dutch?, early 18th century
Included are a soot-rake, shovel, tongs, ladles and a skimmer
Max l. 73.5 cm (2′5″)
M 121-g-1925

(b)
Steel openwork, backed with dyed tortoiseshell
Russian, 17th century
h. 14.4 cm (5½″) w. 10.8 cm (4¼″)
48-1869

(c)
Steel, etched with figures
German, 17th century
h. 10.1 cm (4″) w. 17 cm (3¾″)
744-1893

(d)
Cuir boulli (leather cut and stamped) with wrought iron mounts
Spanish or French, 15th century
h. 10 cm (4″) w. 16.5 cm (6½″)
4318-1857

(e)
Cast iron
German, early 19th century
Known as 'Berlin iron', a type of very fine casting produced by the Prussian Royal Iron Foundry in Berlin, founded in 1804
h. 17.2 cm (6¾″) w. 8 cm (3⅛″)
M 195-1935

(f)
Wrought iron
French?, 15th century
h. 6.4 cm (2½″) w. 9.5 cm (3¾″)
M 248-1912

Plate 12
One of a pair of wall-lights
Iron, wrought and gilded
Italian?, mid-18th century
h. 26 cm (10¼″) w. 25.5 cm (10″)
1550 and 1551 – 1856

Plate 13
Brewer's sign
Wrought iron, painted, and gilded
German, 18th century
Like many trade signs, it incorporates the tools of the trade;
here the maltster's ladle and shovel, encircled by a hop-
wreath.
l. 66 cm (26″) w. 57 cm (22½″)
M 603-1924

Plate 14
Inkstand
Iron, damascened in gold and silver
French, 17th century
h. 5.4 cm (2⅛″) w. 19.7 cm (7¾″)
666-1910

Plate 15 (right)
Tula fireplace
Steel, burnished with applied decoration of gilt copper, brass
and cut steel
Russian, made at the Imperial Arms Factory at Tula near
Moscow, late 18th century. The principal Russian arms
factory at Tula was established in 1705. During the reign of
Catherine the Great (1762-96) it began to produce luxury
items made of steel, blued or burnished, and embellished with
copper and brass, such as chairs, mirrors and dressing tables.
Various pieces now to be seen in the Hermitage Museum,
Leningrad, formerly furnished the old Imperial Palace at
Gatchina. The ornaments of the mantlepiece here include in
the centre a perfume-burner. A letter dated 1806 from an
English girl in Moscow reads: 'have you found out that the
Curiosity from Tula is a machine for perfuming rooms? Its
office I suppose will now be to lie quietly on the steel chimney
piece,' (*The Russian Journals of Martha and Catherine Wilmot*
ed. the Marchioness of Londonderry & HM Hyde, London
1935).
h. 1.87 m (6′1½″) w. 1.46 m (4′10″)
Given by Thomas Harris
M 49-1953

16

Plate 16
Keys
Two kinds of lock were most generally used from the Roman period to the 19th century: the tumbler and the ward lock. With the tumbler lock a fixed pin ensures that only keys with the right bore can be used; this was the type of lock used by the Romans and from the 18th century onwards. With ward locks there is no pin, and it is the pattern of the bit that determines whether the key will turn the lock; this was the type of lock used most in the medieval period.

(a)
Steel, chiselled
English, late 17th century
With the arms of Ralph Stawell, first Baron Somerton (cr. 1682)
l. 12.4 cm ($4\frac{5}{8}''$) w. 4.8 cm ($1\frac{5}{8}''$)
152-1883

(b)
Steel, chiselled
English, 1669
Engraved with the name of Sir Robert Abdy of Albins, Essex
l. 14.6 cm ($5\frac{3}{4}''$) w. 4.4 cm ($1\frac{3}{4}''$)
M 36-1929

(c)
Iron, chiselled
English, 15th century
l. 12 3 cm ($4\frac{7}{8}''$) w. 4 cm ($1\frac{1}{2}''$)
M 117-1909

(d)
Steel, chiselled
French, late 17th century
l. 17.2 cm ($6\frac{3}{4}''$) w. 4.2 cm ($1\frac{5}{8}''$)
2295-1855

(e)
Steel, chiselled
French, late 16th or early 17th century
Known as the Strozzi key, it was alleged to have admitted King Henri III's mistress, Diane de Poitiers, to his private apartments. In fact it probably dates from slightly later; an engraving very close to it appears in *La Fidelle ouverture de l'art du Serrurier,* the locksmithing treatise published by Mathurin Jousse in 1627, in Paris.
l. 11.5 cm ($4\frac{1}{2}''$) w. 5 cm ($2''$)
M 137-1927

(f)
Steel, chiselled
English, 17th century
l. 13.6 cm ($5\frac{3}{8}''$) w. 4.8 cm ($1\frac{5}{8}''$)
1368-1900

(g)
Steel, punched with decoration
English, 18th century
l. 10.1 cm ($4''$) w. 4.4 cm ($1\frac{3}{4}''$)
691-1902

(h)
Latch-key
Steel
English, 19th century
l. 6.4 cm ($2\frac{1}{2}''$) w. 2.2 cm ($\frac{5}{8}''$)
M 340-1917

23

17

Plate 18
Grill in the 'Dutch Kitchen' at the V & A
Cast iron and brass
English, designed by Sir Edward Poynter, dated 1868 and made by Hart Son & Peard
The 'Dutch kitchen' was one of three dining rooms which made up the old restaurant, and was in use, as was the grill, until 1939.

Plate 17
Sword-rest of the Plaisterers' Company
Wrought iron, painted and gilt
English, between 1816 and 1837
In the centre are a sword and mace in saltire, surmounted by the Royal crowns. Scroll work encloses a medallion emblazoned with heraldic shields which are as follows: at the top the Royal Arms as used between 1816 and 1837, in the middle those of the City of London and the Plaisterers' Company; the arms at the bottom are probably those of a former Master of the Company, possibly Thomas Kelly, Alderman and Lord Mayor in 1836.
h. 1.71 m (5′7¼″) w. 75 cm (2′5½″)
383–1896

Plate 19 (right)
Fireplace
Wrought iron, tiles and wood
Scottish, c. 1904
Designed by the architect and designer C.R. Mackintosh (1868-1928) for the Willow Tea Rooms in Glasgow, since demolished.
h. 1.52 m (5′) w. 1.4 m (4′8″)
Circ 244-1963

24

Fig. 14
Gate to the Chantry Chapel of Bishop West, Ely Cathedral
Wrought iron
English, c.1525-33
h. 96 cm (3′2″) w. 1.98 m (6′6″)

14

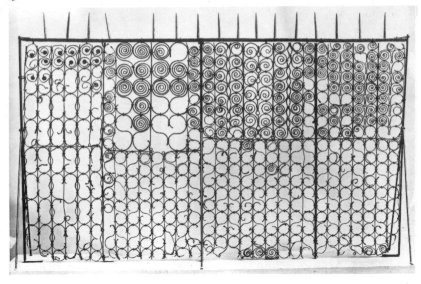

Fig. 15
Screen from Chichester Cathedral
Wrought iron, with traces of the original red
paint
English, 13th century
Patched with a panel of stamped decoration in
the upper left hand corner, similar to that on
the door of Merton College (fig. 35). The
original colour compares with the red painted
railing once around the tomb of Philippa of
Hainault (d. 1369) in Westminster Abbey. The
Chichester screen was removed from the
retrochoir of the cathedral in the 19th century.
h. 2 m (6′6½″) w. 2.98 m (9′11″)
591-1896

Fig. 16
Grille from Winchester Cathedral: detail
Wrought iron
English, a 19th-century copy of the 12th-
century original still in the Cathedral. Perhaps
made originally to protect the shrine of St
Swithun.
h. 1.3 m (4′2″) w. 1.0 m (3′1″)
1891-27

Fig. 17
Grille: detail
Wrought iron
Italian, 17th century
Note the use of both collars and rivets as
joining devices
146-1889

Fig. 18
Grille from the Castle of the Counts of
Flanders, Ghent: detail
Wrought iron, the panels pierced from sheet
iron
Flemish, 16th century
Originally in the chapel
h. 1.13 m (3′8½″) w. 51 cm (1′8″)
601-1883

J Tijou In et del.   B Gentot Sculp

Fig. 19
Design for gates to the Fountain Garden, Hampton Court
Engraving from *The New Booke of Drawings*, English, by Jean
Tijou, 1693
The design and the gates themselves show some differences.
Tijou drew his inspiration from the work of French designers
of a generation or two earlier: Jean de Mortin of c. 1640 and
Hugues Brisville of 1663, and some of his designs derive from
the ironwork of c. 1680 at Versailles.

21

Fig. 20
Gates at Hampton Court
Wrought and embossed iron
English, designed by Jean Tijou in 1693 for William and
Mary's new Fountain Garden at Hampton Court. Prominent
in the design of all the gates are symbols of Great Britain, here
the harp of Ireland.
h. c. 4 m (13′4″) w. c. 4 m (13′4″)

Fig. 21
Satyr mask from the Fountain Garden gates, Hampton Court
Wrought iron, embossed
English, designed by Jean Tijou in 1693
h. 51 cm (1′8″) w. 66 cm (2′2″)
Lent by the Dept. of the Environment

22

Fig. 22
Chancel gates from Salisbury Cathedral
Wrought iron, gilded and painted red
English, designed by Gilbert Scott
c. 1869-72, made by Skidmore & Co.,
Coventry
Scott carried out extensive restorations in
Salisbury Cathedral between 1863-78.
The chancel screen was in place by 1874
and was removed in 1959.
h. 2.26 m (7′5″) w. 2.13 m (7′)
M 4 & a – 1979

23

Fig. 23
Part of the screen from Avila Cathedral,
Spain
Wrought iron, carved and embossed
Spanish, by Juan Frances c. 1520
Another part of this screen is inscribed
with the name Frances, who also did
work in Toledo Cathedral and the
University of Alcara de Henares.
h. 2.79 m (9′2″) w. 56 cm (1′10″)
280-1879

Fig. 24
Screen and gates in the
gardens of New College,
Oxford
Wrought iron
English, by Thomas
Robinson of London, c. 1711

25

26

Fig. 25
Finial from a gate
Wrought iron
English, 18th century
The flowers comprise the national emblems
of Great Britain – rose, thistle, shamrock and
leek – with oak and laurel.
h. 44.5 cm (17″) w. 50.8 cm (18″)
501-1901

Fig. 26
Railings outside the Senate House,
Cambridge: detail
Cast and wrought iron
English, c. 1730
The large uprights are of cast iron, the slender
ones wrought.

27

Fig. 27
Gates to the V & A Huxley
Entrance in Exhibition Road
English, by Starkie Gardner &
Co., c. 1885
Wrought iron
Seen here from the back, the
gates incorporate the mono-
gram SKM, South Kensington
Museum, the name by which
the Museum was known until
1901. The firm of Starkie
Gardner was run by the author
of various books on ironwork,
J. Starkie Gardner.
h. 1.6 m (12′) w. 2.7 m (9′)

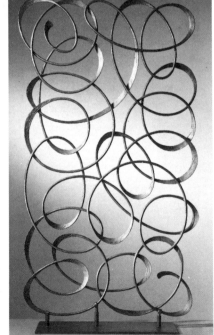

28

29

Fig. 28
Gates to the Town Hall,
Munich
Wrought mild steel
German, by Manfred
Bergmeister 1977
h. 4.5 m
w. 3.9 m

Fig. 29
Grille
Wrought mild steel
German, 1980
Designed and made by Klaus
Walz
h. 2.3 m (7′6½″)
w. 1.2 m (3′11¼″)
M 947-1983

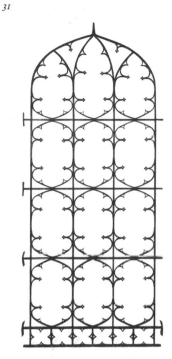

Fig. 30
A window grille from St. Nicholas's Church,
Aachen
Wrought iron
German, 17th century
Note the use of bars of round section, typical of
German work.
h. 1.13m (3′8½″) w. 56.5 cm (22¼″)
991 & a, 992-1893

Fig. 31
Window grille
Wrought iron
Italian, 15th century
h. 1.5 m (4′11″) w. 65.5 cm (2′1¼″)
741-1893

Fig. 32
Window grille
Wrought iron, with applied work, embossed and
engraved
German, 17th century
Note the elaborate bars threaded through each
other.
h. 2.13 m (7′) w. 1.22 m (4′)
5974-1858

Fig. 33
A pair of window grilles
Wrought iron
Italian, 16th century
h. 1.84 m (6′) w. 94 cm (3′1″)
125-1879

33

LIBRARY
College of Marketing & Design
Ph. 742721

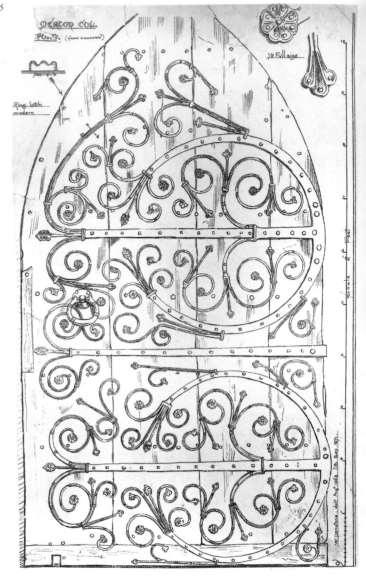

Fig. 34
West door, Durham Cathedral Cloister
Wood and wrought iron
English, late 12th century
h. 2.26 m (7′5″) w. 1.2 m (4′)

Fig. 35
Drawing by W. Denstone, 1868
Door to the Hall of Merton College, Oxford
The ironwork and door are late 13th century; note the
stamped decoration, achieved by hammering punches
into the metal while hot.

36

Fig. 36
Doors from Gannat, Auvergne, France
Wood, with wrought iron hinges
French, 13th century.
h. 2.56 m (8′5″) w. 1.88 m (6′2″)
M 396-1924

37

Fig. 37
Door to the Church of St. Saviour, Dartmouth
Wrought iron and wood
English, 15th century, repaired in 1631.

Fig. 38
Balcony panel
Wrought iron
French, late 17th century.
h. 85 cm (2′9½″) w. 1.8 m (5′11″)
137-1866

Fig. 39
Balcony from No. 1, Impasse des Écuries,
Versailles
Wrought iron, with embossed details,
originally painted light grey
French, c. 1770
The central panel shows the crossed
keys and greyhound supporters of the
Blacksmiths' Guild. The monogram,
apparently two Ls and two Cs, may
represent the initials of Louis XVI and
Jean François Cahon, his blacksmith,
who bought the house in 1770.
h. 99 cm (3′3″) l. 3.4 m (11′2″)
M 51-1909

Fig. 40
Balcony front
Wrought iron
French, mid-18th century
h. 91.5 cm (3′) l. 2.08 m (6′10″)
343-1910

Fig. 41
Balcony front from 12 John Adam Street, Adelphi, London
Cast iron
English, designed, like the house from which it comes, by
James and Robert Adam c. 1773, and probably cast by the
Carron Company. The stucco design on the pilasters echoes
that of the balconies, known as balconettes. Much of the
Adelphi was demolished for redevelopment in 1936.
h. 89 cm (2′11″) w. 1.31 m (4′3½″)
M 429-1936

Fig. 43
Panel for a balcony
Cast iron
French, designed by Hector Guimard, c. 1900
h. 52 cm (1′7¾″) w. 95.5 cm (3′1⅝″)
M 120-1984

Fig. 42
Balcony panel from Gordon Square, London
Cast iron
English, c. 1850
Gordon Square was developed and built by
Thomas Cubitt c. 1850. Similar designs appear
in *The Smith's and Founder's Director* by L.N.
Cottingham (1824).
h. 91.5 cm (3′) w. 68.7 cm (2′3⅛″)
M 23-1958

LIBRARY
College of Marketing & Design
No. 747721

44

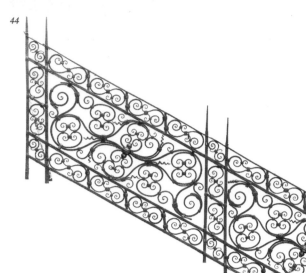

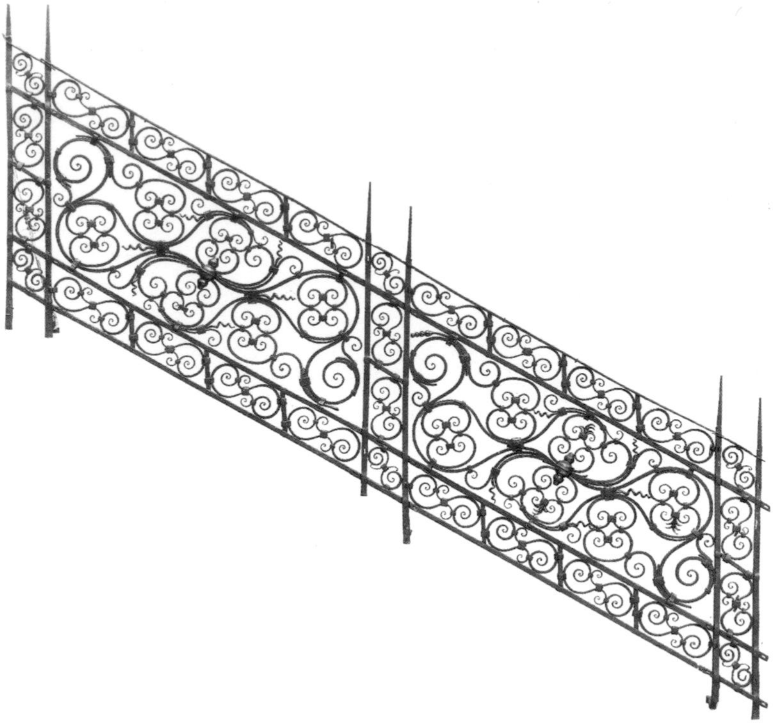

Fig. 44
Staircase balustrade
Wrought iron
Italian, 17th century
h. 84 cm (2′9″) l. 3 m (10′)
660-1888

45

Fig. 45
Staircase balustrade
Wrought iron, embossed and originally
painted and gilded
Italian, from Venice, 17th century
h. 1.26 m (4′2″) l. 3.15 m (10′6″)
5966-1857

46

Fig. 46
Top Row
Balusters from staircases
All are English
(a) Wrought iron, with a cast
brass rosette plate – 18th century
h. 1.04 m (3′5″) w. 17 cm (6¾″)
Private collection

(b) Cast iron, painted olive
green
Mid-19th century
h. 1.1 m (3′7¼″) w. 17 cm (6½″)
M 172-1978

(c) Cast iron, about 1900
h. 84 cm (2′9″) w. 18.5 cm (7¼″)
M186-1978

Bottom Row
Balusters from staircases
All are English, of wrought iron,
and date from the 18th century
(d) h. 98 cm (3′2½″) w. 24 cm (9¾″)
411-1911

(e) With cast brass embellishments
h. 96 cm (3′1¾″) w. 13.8 cm (5½″)
Circ 308-1910

(f) h. 93 cm (3′½″) w. 18.5 cm
(7¼″)
M 60-1943

(g) With cast brass embellishments
h. 1.97 m (3′6″) w. 27 cm (10½″)
657-1888

(h) From 12 Charles Street,
London, SW1
h. 97.5 cm (3′2¼″) w. 24.5 cm
(9½″)
213-1924

(j) From Foley House, Portland
Place, London
Built c. 1774
h. 86.5 cm (2′10″) w. 25 cm (9¾″)
935a-1928

37

Fig. 47
Stove from Compton Place, Eastbourne
Cast iron
English, late-18th century
Probably designed by Robert Adam and made by the Carron Company.
Similar stoves designed by Adam are at Kedleston Hall, Derbys.
h. 1.7 m (5′7″) w. 53 cm (1′9″)
M 3-1920

Fig. 48
Trade card of Henry Jackson, London
Engraving
English, c. 1777
This was the advertising leaflet of its day, and shows the variety of fireplaces and stoves available. Register stoves can be seen on the lower left and right.
British Museum, Dept. of Prints and Drawings, Banks Collection (no. D 2 107)

Fig. 49
Firegrate
Cast iron
English, possibly designed by the Adam brothers and cast by the Carron Company, c. 1780. The neo-classical motifs are typical features of the Adams' work.
h. 67.3 cm (2′2½″) w. 1.36 (4′5½″)
M 425-1936

50

Fig. 50
Firegrate *The Rape of Proserpine*
Cast iron with cast bronze firedogs
English, designed by Alfred Stevens
(1817-75); made by Henry Hoole & Co of
Sheffield, c. 1850. Alfred Stevens was
primarily a sculptor and designer but was
employed by Hoole & Co to design grates
for the Great Exhibition of 1851, at which
this was exhibited. He also designed
radiator grilles and dining room tables in
cast iron for the V & A.
h. 89 cm (2′ 11″) w. 99 cm (3′ 3″)
4029-1853

51

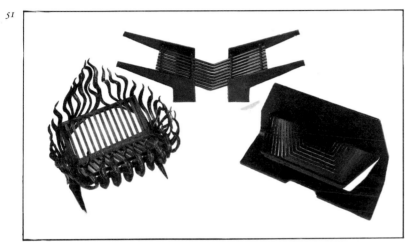

Fig. 51
Firegrates
(a) Wrought mild steel
English, by Antony Robinson, 1979
Robinson's work includes the spectacular
gates in the medieval Great Hall at
Winchester, made 1981-3.
h. 56 cm (1′ 10″) w. 54.5 cm (1′ 10″)
M 75-1979

(b) Wrought mild steel
English, by James Horrobin 1981
Horrobin made the gates to one of the
entrances to the V & A Ironwork Gallery in
1981-2.
h. 30 cm (1′) w. 1.1 cm (3′ 7″)
M 31-1981

(c) Mild steel plate, cut with an oxyacetylene cutter
English, by Stuart Hill 1982
h. 37 cm (1′ 2½″) w. 68.5 cm (2′ 3″)
Private Collection

39

52

Fig. 52
The Capel Garmon firedog
Wrought iron
Celtic, c. 50 BC – 50 AD
Found in a peat bog in Denbighshire in
1852. It would originally have been one of a
pair, in a hearth positioned centrally.
h. 75 cm (2′5½″) w. 106.7 cm (3′6″)
Cardiff, National Museum of Wales

53

Fig. 53
Firedogs in wrought iron
(a) English, designed by C. Ashbee and
made by the Guild of Handicraft, 1900-05,
with a copper and brass rosette as finial
h. 40.5 cm (1′4″) w. 24 cm (9½″)
Circ 295-1959

(b) French, stamped 'MADE IN FRANCE. E.
BRANDT', c. 1930
The grape-motif finial is partly embellished
with bronze
h. 72 cm (2′4½″) w. 32 cm (1′1½″)
M 88-1979

(c) Italian?, late 15th century
h. 59 cm (1′11¼″) w. 51 cm (1′8″)
M 182-1926

(d) French, 17th century?, from Dijon
The hooks at the front were to hold spits,
the bracket at the top to hold a flask
h. 82.5 cm (2′8½″) w. 43.5 cm (1′5″)
M 656-1905

Fig. 55
Firedogs
Wrought mild steel
American, designed and made by Albert Paley 1981
h. 60 cm (1′ 11¾″) w. 60 cm (1′ 11¾″)
Private collection

Fig. 54
Firedogs in cast iron
(Although shown here singly, they were used in pairs, one on each side of the hearth, the logs being laid across them)

(a) English, 17th century
From Hythe, Kent
h. 27 cm (10½″) w. 27 cm (10½″)
4434-1857

(b) English, inscribed 'TP' and dated 1637, from Barham Court, Kent
Decorated with the buckle badge of the Pelhams
h. 48 cm (1′ 7″) w. 40 cm (1′ 3¾″)
M 979-1926

(c) French, 16th century
h. 56 cm (1′ 10″) w. 50 cm (1′ 7½″)
735-1895

(d) German, late-15th century
From Rott, near Cornelymünster
h. 66 cm (2′ 2″) w. 45.5 cm (1′ 6″)
1016-1893

(e) English, 17th century
With the initials 'WI'
h. 47 cm (1′ 6½″) w. 56 cm (1′ 10″)
899-1901

Firebacks

These protected the back wall of the chimney from the flames and projected the heat forward. References to them occur from at least the 15th century in England, but no dated examples are known before the 16th century.

Fig. 56
Fireback
Cast-iron
English, probably Sussex, mid-16th century
The birds may allude to Nicholas Fowle who had a furnace and forge at Riverhall, Wadhurst, Kent, from about 1547 (both of which had become ruins by 1664). This shape is the simplest and probably the earliest found in firebacks.
h. 53.2 cm (1′9″) w. 77.5 cm (2′6″) d. c.2.5 cm (1″)
Given by Lady Dorothy Nevill
M 120–1914

57

Fig. 57
'Armada' fireback
Cast iron
English, probably Sussex, dated 1588
So called only because its date coincides with that of the defeat of the Armada. The initials IFC are those of the person for whom it was made, rather than those of the maker. Modern reproductions of this design are common.
h. 87 cm (2′10″) w. 1.04 m (3′5″) d. 3.8 cm (1½″)
M 77–1957

58

Fig. 58
Fireback
Cast iron
English, dated 1604
With the Royal arms of James I, and the lion and unicorn as supporters. James was the first King of England to use the unicorn on his coat-of-arms.
h. 58.5 cm (23″) w. 77.5 cm (2′6½″)
M 44-1912

Fig. 59
Stove-plate
Cast iron, inscribed 'HISTORIA. VON. DER. HOCHZEIT. ZU CANA IN
GALILEA. JOHAN. 2'
German, late 16th century
The subject, the marriage feast at Cana, was popular on
German stove-plates, which often depicted Biblical subjects.
h. 53.5 cm (21″) w. 70 cm (2′3½″)
319-1897

Fig. 60
Fire-back
Cast iron, showing Moses and the serpent in the wilderness
German or Dutch, 17th century
The shape of the fireback and the elaborate floral border are
typical Dutch and German features.
h. 91 cm (2′11¾″) w. 65.5 cm (2′1¾″)
291-1893

Fig. 61
Fireback
Cast iron
English, mid-17th century
This design was apparently first used under James I and VI to
signify the union under him of the crowns of England,
Scotland and Ireland. The initials may be those of Charles I,
or Charles II (for whom the oak would be a particularly
appropriate allusion to his famous escape in 1651, after the
battle of Worcester, by hiding in the Boscobel oak tree).
h. 76 cm (2′6″) w. 90 cm (2′11½″) d. 3.1 cm (1¼″)
255-1906

62a

62b

Door-knockers

The oldest surviving door-knockers date from the early medieval period, and are found on church doors, generally made of bronze. Later in the medieval period wrought iron was used, although bronze was again much used in the Renaissance. The largest numbers of English door-knockers to survive date from the 19th century, and are of cast iron.

Fig. 62

(a) Wrought iron
French, 15th century
l. 28 cm (11″) w. 12.5 cm (5″)
2615-1856

(b) Wrought iron
Italian?, 15th century
l. 16 cm (6¼″) w. 5.6 cm (2⅜″)
518-1895

(c) Wrought iron
French, 17th century
l. 24.5 cm (9⅝″) w. 23 cm (9″)
1219-1855

(d) Wrought iron, embossed
South German, 17th century
l. 49.5 cm (19½″) w. 21.5 cm (8½″)
M 510-1911

62c

62d

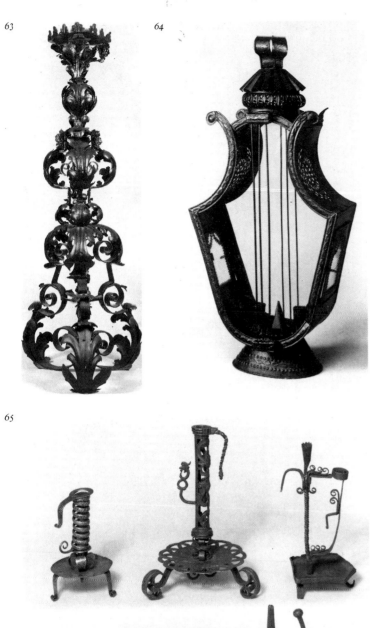

Fig. 63
Standing candlestick
Wrought iron, embossed
Venetian, 17th century
h. 1.75 m (5′9″) w. 61 cm (2′)
439-1882

Fig. 64
Lantern
Sheet iron, pierced and embossed, and glass
English or French, early 19th century
It would originally have held two candles.
h. 43 cm (1′5″) w. 22.8 cm (9″)
M 293-1975

Candlesticks
Early candlesticks consisted of spikes or prick-
ets on which the candle was impaled. These
were gradually superseded by the socket type
of holder, often adjustable in height, as nos.
1029–1893 and 674–1872 here. Rushlights were a
cheaper form of candle, made by dipping dried
and peeled rushes in molten tallow.

Fig. 65

(a) Wrought iron
German, 18th century?
h. 17.2 cm (6¾″)
1029-1893

(b) Wrought iron
German, dated 1672
Inscribed 'Got geb uns ewige liecht'
h. 28.5 cm (11¼″)
674-1872

(c) Wrought iron
German, 16th century?
h. 25.4 cm (10″)
M 16-1945

(d) Rushlight-holder
Wrought iron, engraved
Italian, 17th century
h. 15.9 cm (6¼″)
1038-1893

(e) Rushlight-holder
Wrought iron
English, 18th century
h. 21.6 cm (8½″)
M 383-1917

Fig. 66
Casket
Steel, chiselled and polished
Italian or French, made for the Duc de Medici
c.1609-21, either by an Italian, Gasparo Mola,
or a Frenchman, François Lemaistre. Inside the
lid is the Medici coat of arms, under a grand-
ducal crown. The decoration includes the
figures of Mars and Minerva.
h. 25.5 cm (10″) w. 18.5 cm (7¼″)
M 95-1960

Fig. 67
Coffer
Wrought iron
Flemish, early 16th century
h. 68.5 cm (2′3″) w. 1.1 m (3′9″)
M 295-1912

Fig. 68
Lift-cage panel from Selfridges, London
Wrought iron and beaten tin plate, fixed to
plywood and painted gold and bronze
French, designed by Edgar Brandt c.1922-28. In
1928 Brandt supplied Selfridges with four pairs of
lifts, each with three panels like this. They were
removed during the modernisation in the 1960s.
h. 1.94 m (6′4½″) w. 1.26 m (4′1½″)
Circ. 719-1971

Fig. 69
Balconies at no. 11, Sq. Ambiorix, Brussels
Wrought iron
Belgian, designed, like the house, by Gustave
Strauven (1878-1919) in 1903, for the painter de
Saint-Cyr. Strauven worked for Horta between
1896 and 1898.

Fig. 70
Brussels: interior of the Musée
Horta, by Victor Horta
Wrought iron, 1898
The house was built in the Rue
Américaine by Horta for his
own use. Many other exam-
ples of his architecture and
distinctive ironwork can still
be seen in Brussels.

Fig. 71
Coal exchange, Lower Thames Street, London: detail
English, by J.B. Bunning, 1847-49
Cast iron, with a glass dome
The building had three tiers of offices, under a dome; it was demolished in 1962 as
part of a road widening scheme still incomplete. A cable pattern ornamented the
iron structural members, ceilings and balustrades. Several sections of the building
were saved and are in the V & A and Science Museums.

BACK ENDPAPER *(left)*
A page from the MacFarlane & Co.,
Catalogue of Castings, 1882-3, showing the possibilities of cast iron for and
in a building. From their 'Saracen
Foundry' in Glasgow, MacFarlanes
exported cast iron all over the world,
including entire buildings, a bank to
Madras, bandstands to Adelaide.
They provided some of the ironwork
for the V & A, such as the balustrading and stairs in the Library.

BACK ENDPAPER *(right)*
A page from the Catalogue of
Barbezat & Cie. of Paris 1858.
Wrought iron had been used earlier
for the grave-crosses which took the
place of tombstones in southern
Germany. In France and Germany
these cast iron crosses became popular
for a while in the 19th century.

Leabharlanna Átha Cliath